SCOTLAND

A MISCELLANY

Compiled by Julia Skinner

THE FRANCIS FRITH COLLECTION

www.francisfrith.com

First published in the United Kingdom in 2013 by The Francis Frith Collection®

ISBN 978-1-84546-580-3

Text and Design copyright The Francis Frith Collection®
Photographs copyright The Francis Frith Collection® except where indicated.

The Frith® photographs and the Frith® logo are reproduced under licence from
Heritage Photographic Resources Ltd, the owners of the Frith® archive and trademarks.
'The Francis Frith Collection', 'Francis Frith' and 'Frith' are registered trademarks of
Heritage Photographic Resources Ltd.

British Library Cataloguing in Publication Data

Did You Know? Scotland - A Miscellany
Compiled by Julia Skinner

The Francis Frith Collection
6 Oakley Business Park,
Wylye Road, Dinton,
Wiltshire SP3 5EU
Tel: +44 (0) 1722 716 376
Email: info@francisfrith.co.uk

www.francisfrith.com

Printed and bound in England
Contains material sourced from responsibly managed forests

Front Cover: **LOCH ACHRAY, THE TROSSACHS CHURCH 1871** L89001p
Frontispiece: **ARRAN, THE CASTLE AND LOCH RANZA c1890** A93001
Contents: **ROTHESAY, THE PIER 1897** 39836

The colour-tinting is for illustrative purposes only, and is not intended to be historically accurate

CONTENTS

SCOTLAND
INTRODUCTION

Fàilte gu Alba – *Welcome to Scotland*

Before the country we now call Scotland had that name, it was known variously as Caledonia, Alba (its Gaelic name) and Pictland, after the 'Picti', or 'painted people', who lived there, called that by the Romans because of their custom of tattooing themselves. The Romans occupied Britain from AD43 until the early fifth century, but despite several military campaigns they never managed to conquer the land they called Caledonia.

From the early sixth century onwards, Gaelic-speaking people from Ireland began to migrate to the west coast of Scotland. The area where they first settled was known as 'Earra-Ghàidheal', meaning 'coastline of the Gael', later corrupted to Argyll. These Gaelic people were the original 'Scots', their name deriving from the Latin name of 'Scoti' that the Romans used for the Irish Gaels, meaning pirates or raiders. Many Scottish placenames derive from their Gaelic language, and also commonly used names for topographical features, such as 'loch' for a lake or sea inlet, 'ben' for a mountain, and 'glen' for a valley.

STIRLING, THE BRUCE STATUE AND THE WILLIAM WALLACE MONUMENT ON ABBEY CRAIG 1899 44680

'Brave are the hearts that beat beneath Scottish skies.'
(From 'Scotland the Brave' by Cliff Hanley, 1922-1999)

The first king of Scotland is traditionally said to be Kenneth MacAlpin, whose father was King Alpin of the Scots and whose mother was a Pictish princess; he united the kingdoms of the Picts and Scots and ruled as Kenneth I from AD843 to 858. Subsequently the language and customs of the Picts gradually disappeared and were replaced by those of the Scots, and eventually the name of 'Pictland' was superseded by 'Scotland', as the kingdom of the Scots grew and acquired control of other territories.

Scotland has had a turbulent history with its English neighbour, but has never been conquered. Edward I of England claimed overlordship of Scotland in 1296 but English rule was resisted by two great names in Scotland's struggle for independence, first by William Wallace and then by Robert the Bruce, who in 1314 claimed the important victory over the English army of Edward II at Bannockburn. In 1603 James VI of Scotland inherited the English throne after the death of his distant cousin Elizabeth I and also became James I of England, uniting the two Crowns. Although he then transferred his court to London, Scotland kept its own government for another century. When Scotland did eventually incorporate politically with England under the Act of Union of 1707 it was by treaty, not conquest. Under the terms of the Treaty of Union the Scottish Parliament signed away its separate existence in exchange for 45 seats in the Westminster Parliament, free trade with England, and the retention of legal and ecclesiastical freedom, although this was bitterly opposed by many Scots. As he put his signature to the treaty, the Earl of Seafield famously commented: 'Now, there's ane end of ane auld song.'

However, the old song had not ended after all. In 1998 the Scotland Act was passed by the United Kingdom Parliament in response to a growing movement for a return to direct Scottish control over domestic affairs, and in 1999 the Scottish Parliament was reconvened as a devolved legislature with responsibility for most laws specific to Scotland and authority over home affairs – the first time it had met for nearly 300 years.

SCOTS WORDS AND PHRASES

'Brae' – a slope, or small hill.

'Braw' – very good.

'Breeks' – trousers (originally breeches).

'Burn' – a stream.

'But and ben' – an old term for a small two-roomed cottage.

'Corbie' – a crow.

'Cuddy' – a donkey or horse.

'Dree' – to suffer or endure.

'Dreich' – dull or dreary.

'Gae' or **'gang'** – to go.

'Glaikit' – foolish.

'Gloaming' – twilight, dusk.

'Greet' – to cry, as in **'a greetin' bairn'** – a crying child.

'Ken' – to know.

'Kirk' – a church.

'Maun' – must.

'Muckle' – big, great, large.

'Pleuch' – plough.

'Sea-maw' – a seagull.

'Sleekit' – cunning, sly.

'Stoochie' – a fuss, disturbance.

'Wean' and **'bairn'** – a small child.

'Wee' – small, little.

'Weel-kent' – well-known, familiar.

'Blythe may we a' be, ill may we never see' – a traditional toast.

HAUNTED CASTLES

Scotland is famous for its castles, many of which are reputed to be haunted. Here are just a few:

Edinburgh Castle is said to be haunted by a phantom drummer who marches on the battlements beating out a rhythm – the sound of his spectral drumbeat warns of bad news.

The rather startling shade of a woman holding her decapitated head is said to roam Drumlanrig Castle, near Thornhill in Dumfriesshire. She is thought to be the phantom of Lady Anne Douglas, but no one knows why she is headless. Drumlanrig is also haunted by an unusual ghost in the form of a large yellow monkey, which is only seen in one particular room.

A mysterious 'Green Lady' haunts Crathes Castle, near Banchory in Aberdeenshire. She only manifests in a room in its oldest part, the double tower, which is called the Green Lady's Room because of her many appearances there. She glides across the room to the fireplace, where she stoops down to pick up a baby then fades from sight, holding the child in her arms – and during restoration work in the building some years ago, the skeletons of a woman and baby were discovered beneath the hearth. Despite the removal of the remains from their place of hiding, the Green Lady still haunts the room.

Duns Castle in Berwickshire has been the home of the Hay family since 1696. It is said to be haunted by the shade of 18-year-old Alexander Hay, a Cornet in the 16th Light Dragoons who was killed fighting at the Battle of Waterloo in 1815. His body was never found on the battlefield, but his spirit seems to have returned home – his apparition has been seen in several rooms of the castle, dressed in full military uniform.

Scotland miscellany

The part of the British Isles that is now Scotland was once completely separate from the rest of Britain, and about 600 million years ago was actually attached to the North American landmass. Then it broke free and drifted west, ending up north of what is now England. Eventually the two landmasses collided and joined together with monumental force. The stresses and straining of their joining, together with volcanic eruptions on the western seaboard, helped produce many of the islands of the Hebrides, Orkneys and Shetlands and the bedrock of much of the coastal region of north-west Scotland, especially around Lochinver – it is here that the oldest rock in Britain is found, Lewisian Gneiss, a hard metamorphic rock around 3,000 million years old, formed from igneous rocks that have been subjected to extremely high pressure and intense heat.

Over subsequent millennia, erosion, Ice Age glaciers, geological movement and more volcanic activity helped produce the vast mountains and deep glens of Scotland's landscape. A remnant of that turbulent period is the Highland Boundary Fault Line, a deep fracture formed millions of years ago from the splitting and folding of the earth's crust, where the rock has not settled and there are still occasional earth tremors; it runs diagonally from the Firth of Clyde in the south-west to Stonehaven in the north-east, and traditionally separates the Highland area of Scotland from the Lowlands.

Fascinating relics of Scotland's prehistoric past can be found on the seashore at Crail, on the east coast of Fife near Anstruther, in the form of fossilised tree stumps, the petrified remains of a prehistoric forest that grew there in the Carboniferous period about 335 million years ago. The trees were growing in what was then a sandy swamp; the ground later solidified into sandstone, on which the preserved tracks of a giant millipede-like creature (Arthropleura) that once crawled between the trees can be seen – scientists estimate this prehistoric monster insect was about 4½ feet long!

ORKNEY, HUT 1, SKARA BRAE 1954 O108026

The most northerly point of mainland Scotland is Easter Head on the peninsula of Dunnet Head in Caithness, about 11 miles west-northwest of John o' Groats – the village at the northern end of the longest distance between two inhabited points on mainland Britain, Land's End in Cornwall being the southern point. It is named after Jan de Groote, a Dutchman who settled there in the late 15th century and ran a ferry to the Orkney Islands.

Scotland's Northern Isles are the two island groups of the Orkneys and Shetlands. Both are rich in archaeological remains, including the extraordinary Neolithic village of Skara Brae on the Orkneys. The site was buried under sand for over 40 centuries until a storm exposed a number of stone buildings, which radiocarbon dating proved to date from the late Neolithic period, inhabited between 3,200 and 2,200BC. Because the sand had protected the buildings for so long, they are remarkably well preserved. The houses all share the same basic design of a large, square room with a central hearth and what appears to be a dresser with shelves, made out of stone, on the wall opposite the doorway.

SCOTLAND

Mainland Scotland has around 6,000 miles of coastline, off which are 790 islands of which 96 were listed as inhabited in the 2001 Census. The most remote inhabited island in the British Isles is Fair Isle, midway between the Orkney and Shetland Islands and 23 miles from the nearest land, which is administratively part of the Shetlands. The island has given its name to the intricate Fair Isle knitting technique of creating patterns with multiple colours, which is probably of Norse origin – the Orkney and Shetland islands were settled by Norsemen in the 9th century and ruled by Norway or Demark until they passed to Scotland in 1468, when Christian I of Norway pawned them in lieu of a dowry on his daughter's marriage to James III; the money was never paid, and in 1471 the Northern Isles were formally annexed to the Crown of Scotland.

Knitting has been an important industry on the Shetlands for centuries, as the fine wool of the local sheep has a light, soft texture more suitable for knitwear (including delicate lacy shawls) than woven cloth. However, the 'Shetland' name has been much plagiarised by manufacturers around the world, so a certification trademark, 'The Shetland Lady', has been registered for use only on knitwear genuinely made on the Shetland Islands.

The remotest part of the British Isles is St Kilda, an archipelago of four islands way out in the Atlantic 40 miles west-northwest of North Uist in the Outer Hebrides. St Kilda was inhabited until 1930, when the remaining 36 islanders asked to be evacuated to the mainland. St Kilda is now a World Heritage Site cared for by the National Trust for Scotland, and is an important breeding ground for seabirds such as gannets and puffins.

A SHETLAND KNITTER c1890 A001086

Scotland

Although the Sutherland region of the Scottish Highlands is the northernmost part of mainland Scotland, its name actually means 'southern land' – this derives from the era of Viking rule and settlement of the Orkney and Shetland islands, when the Norsemen saw this region as being south of their territories. The dramatic name of Cape Wrath, at the extreme north-west point of Sutherland, comes from the Norse word 'hvraf', meaning 'turning point', as this was where the Vikings turned south on their way to the Hebridean islands and the Isle of Man, which they also held from the 9th century until 1266, when these territories were purchased by the Scottish Crown under the Treaty of Perth.

Sutherland is now one of the most sparsely populated regions in Britain as a result of the Highland Clearances of the 19th century, when landlords drove thousands of crofters from their land to use it more profitably for large-scale sheep farming. A sad testament to those times can be seen on the east window of the church at Croick, about ten miles up Stratchcarron to the west of the village of Ardgay, where messages scratched on the glass commemorate the plight of around 90 local people evicted from their lands at Glencalvie in 1845, who lived in temporary shelters in the churchyard before leaving the area.

The highest sea cliffs on mainland Britain as well as Britain's highest free-falling waterfall are found in the spectacular scenery of Sutherland. The waterfall is Eas Coul Aulin (a corruption of its Gaelic name meaning 'waterfall of the beautiful tresses'), to the east of the A894 near Loch Assynt. It has a sheer drop of around 650 feet (200 metres) – almost four times the height of Niagara Falls in America. The cliffs are at Clò Mòr, about 4 miles east along the coast from Cape Wrath, and at their highest point they rise to a vertigo-inducing 921 feet (281 metres) above the sea.

The highest mountain in the British Isles is in Scotland, Ben Nevis, which is located at the western end of the Grampian mountains near Fort William. Known to both locals and visitors as 'The Ben', at 4,409 feet (1,344 metres) high it is very popular with climbers. The name of the mountain is an Anglicised version of the Scottish Gaelic 'Beinn Nibheis'. 'Beinn' means 'mountain', but there are several possible meanings of 'Nibheis' – it is most commonly translated as 'malicious', but it may derive from 'nèamh-bhathais', meaning 'heavens' (from 'nèamh') and 'top of a man's head' (from 'bathais'), giving a more romantic interpretation of 'the mountain with its head in the clouds', or perhaps 'mountain of Heaven'.

Of the 88,795 square miles that make up the landmass of Great Britain (including Northern Ireland and various island groups), 30,414 square miles is Scotland – roughly one third of the total area. However, according to the 2011 Census, the population of Scotland is only 8.4% of the total UK figure – 5,295,000.

BEN NEVIS FROM CORPACH
1890 B267001

SCOTLAND

One of the most spectacular megalithic monuments in Scotland is the magnificent Standing Stones of Callanish (or Calanais, in its Gaelic version) on the Isle of Lewis in the Outer Hebrides, often called 'Scotland's Stonehenge'. This mysterious ancient monument was erected between 2,900 and 2,600BC and is one of the most complete prehistoric stone circles in Europe, comprising around 50 standing stones of local Lewisian Gneiss rock. An inner circle of 13 primary stones surrounding a massive central stone is approached by a long avenue of stones to the north with shorter stone rows to the east, south, and west, in a layout resembling a distorted Celtic cross. The tallest stone marks the entrance to a chambered cairn tomb where human remains have been discovered, which was a later addition to the site.

There are many theories about the purpose of the Callanish Stones. Some people think they formed a calendar system based on the position of the moon, or were connected with rituals relating to the moon and a range of hills of the Pairc district of south-east Lewis whose outline against the sky resembles the form of a woman lying on her back – local people call her the 'Sleeping Beauty', or 'Cailleach na Mòinteach' in Gaelic, which translates as 'The Old Woman of the Moors'; Mòr Mhonadh forms her knees, Guaineamol forms her breasts, and Sidhean an Airgid forms her head and face. The 'Sleeping Beauty' can be seen from many parts of the island, including Callanish, where during the major lunar standstill the moon appears to rise from her 'breasts' as if reborn, skims the horizon and then appears between the stones of the central circle before setting. The lunar standstill is a celestial event that occurs once every 18.61 years when the moon rises at its least northerly and sets at its most southerly point; at this time the moon's position changes from high in the sky to low on the horizon, when an optical illusion makes it appear very close and large, a phenomenon that is seen to greatest effect the further north you are; the next time this happens will be in 2025.

'Love makes the world go round? Not at all.
Whisky makes it go round twice as fast.'
(Compton Mackenzie, 'Whisky Galore', 1947)

Eriskay is a tiny island in the Outer Hebrides that became famous after the SS 'Politician' ran aground there in 1941 with a cargo of 28,000 cases of malt whisky. The delighted islanders 'salvaged' much of its cargo in a furtive series of well-organised but illegal looting operations, to the fury of the local customs officer. The event inspired Compton Mackenzie's novel 'Whisky Galore' and the subsequent 1949 Ealing comedy film of the book, although it was filmed on location on the nearby island of Barra, not Eriskay.

The name 'whisky' comes from the Gaelic 'uisge-beatha', meaning 'water of life', which was corrupted to 'usqua' or 'usky'. No one knows exactly when the Scots learnt their art of distilling whisky, but the first official record of it is from the late 15th century. Many factors give the whisky made in Scotland its distinctive flavour and bouquet, but the combination of the country's cold climate, soft water, fine barley and fragrant peat used as fuel in the malting and distilling processes all have a profound effect, as the environment in which whisky is produced has as much bearing on its character as how long it is stored and left to mature. Whisky is produced by many distilleries throughout the Highlands and Islands, but particularly in the 'whisky triangle' around the River Spey; the Inner Hebridian island of Islay is also famous for the single malt whiskies produced at eight distilleries there, all with a distinctive peaty character.

The 'water of life' made in Scotland is known as Scotch whisky in the rest of the world, or just 'Scotch'. And whisky made in Scotland is always spelled without an 'e' – whiskey with an 'e' is the Irish stuff!

Scotland

The Inner Hebrides lie closer to the Scottish mainland than the Outer Hebrides, and include the islands of Canna, Eigg, Iona, Islay, Jura, Muck, Mull, Raasay, Rum and Skye.

The largest island is Mull, off which are two small islands that have become world-famous, Staffa and Iona.

The tiny uninhabited island of Staffa is famous for its sea caves and basaltic rock formations, the best-known of which is Fingal's Cave, where smooth black columns of basalt rise from the sea like great organ pipes. The cave is renowned for its acoustics and earned its Gaelic name of 'An Uaimh Bhinn', 'the melodious cave', from the sound of the sea echoing through its depths. It was also immortalised in music after the composer Felix Mendelssohn visited Staffa in 1829 and composed his concert overture 'The Hebrides' as a tribute to the beauty and atmosphere he found there, a piece popularly known as 'Fingal's Cave'.

Off the south-west of Mull is the island of Iona, often called 'the cradle of Scottish Christianity'. In AD563 St Columba chose Iona as the site for a monastery from where he could carry out his missionary work to the pagan Picts, after coming to Scotland from Ireland. From there, St Columba and his missionaries converted a large part of Scotland to Christianity. Iona was an important spiritual centre of the Kingdom of Alba following its establishment in the 9th century and many of its early kings were buried there, including Kenneth MacAlpin. In 1203 a new Benedictine monastery was founded on the island, with its abbey church built on the site of St Columba's original church. Iona Abbey lasted until the Reformation, but then fell into ruin. In 1899 the 8th Duke of Argyll presented the abbey ruins to the Church of Scotland, which undertook extensive restoration of the site. Iona Abbey was substantially rebuilt in the mid 20th century by the Iona Community, and is now an ecumenical place of worship. The abbey continues to be an intensely spiritual place, and around 200,000 pilgrims visit Iona each year.

Oban is the ferry port for the islands on the west coast of Scotland, sited on the mainland near the Isle of Mull. The strange circular building overlooking the town on the right of this view is McCaig's Tower, an unfinished replica of the Colosseum in Rome which was built by local banker and Oban citizen John Stuart McCaig in the 1890s as a memorial to his family. Oban is a popular place for scuba diving in Scotland because of the variety of marine life and numerous shipwrecks found in the crystal-clear waters around the bay, including the well-preserved wreck of the SS 'Breda', a cargo ship sunk by German bombers in 1940. One diving couple even got married on the deck of the SS 'Breda' – but they had to provide diving lessons for the minister first!

Beside Loch Sunart, north of Oban, is Strontian, which gave its name to the carbonate mineral of strontianite as well as the chemical element of strontium. Lead was mined in the hills north of the village in the 18th century, and it was in the lead mines there that strontianite was first discovered in 1790, from which strontium is extracted.

OBAN, FROM THE SOUTH WEST 1901 47506

15

Scotland

The nine of diamonds in a pack of playing cards is known as 'The Curse of Scotland', but no one is exactly sure why. One theory is that the pattern of nine diamonds resembles the armorial bearings of Sir John Dalrymple, Earl of Stair and Secretary of State over Scotland, and the card may have got this name because of his part in sanctioning the notorious Massacre of Glencoe in 1692, when troops under a Campbell commander attacked three settlements of the MacDonald clan, killing over forty people. The massacre was widely condemned and particularly shocking because the troops had billeted with the MacDonalds and enjoyed their hospitality for twelve days before launching their attack.

The attack on the MacDonalds of Glencoe was ordered as retribution for the alleged failure of their chieftain to swear allegiance to William III (1689-1702) by the time appointed by the government, partly because he was delayed by bad weather. King William had come to the throne in the 'Glorious Revolution' of 1688-69, when dissatisfaction with James II (of England, also James VII of Scotland) over his absolutionist monarchy and Catholicism led a group of English nobles to invite the Protestant Prince William of the Dutch state of Orange to take the throne as joint monarch with his wife, King James's daughter Mary. King James fled into exile and a Convention of the Estates in Scotland in 1689 decided he had forfeited the Scottish crown and recognised the new king, but many people in Scotland still supported him as the true monarch in the Stuart line of descent from his grandfather, James VI of Scotland, who had also become James I of England in 1603 when the two Crowns were united; his supporters were known as 'Jacobites', from 'Jacobus', the Latin form of James.

For nearly 60 years there were a series of Jacobite attempts to restore first King James to the throne and then (after his death in 1701) his son James Edward Stuart, known as the 'Old Pretender' by non Jacobites. The most serious was the last, of 1745-46, when an army of mainly Scottish Highlanders was led by James Edward Stuart's son, Prince Charles, better known as 'Bonnie Prince Charlie'. This ended in bloody defeat in 1746 at Culloden Moor near Inverness, the last pitched battle on British soil, and the effective end of the Jacobite cause. The defeated prince fled for his life around the Highlands and Western Isles before escaping to France, and lived out the rest of his days in Italy.

After Culloden it was treason to support the Stuart claim to the throne, so Jacobites showed their allegiance in covert ways, such as drinking a toast to the 'king over the sea' over a symbolic bowl of water, using glasses engraved with secret Jacobite motifs. A fascinating example of hidden Jacobite support is the 'secret portrait' table in the West Highland Museum at Fort William, whose top is painted with a meaningless swirl of colours that form into a picture of Bonnie Prince Charlie when reflected onto the side of a curved and polished vessel placed in the centre of the table, such as a goblet or decanter.

After the 1745-46 Jacobite rising, the government sought to break up the Highland clan system by banning various aspects of its culture; amongst other things, an Act of Proscription of 1746 banned the wearing of clan tartans and other forms of 'Highland Dress' for 36 years until it was repealed in 1782. Off the west coast south of Oban is the island of Seil, where the name of the Tigh an Truish pub is Gaelic for 'House of the Trousers', a reminder of when wearing kilts was banned. When the Seil islanders went across the water to the mainland, it was there that they changed from their kilts into the hated trews before continuing on their journey.

SCOTLAND

'Nowhere beats the heart so kindly as beneath the tartan plaid.'
(William Edmondstoune Aytoun, 1813-1865)

The earliest example of tartan cloth in Scotland was discovered in Falkirk in 1934, when workmen found a large hoard of Roman coins in a clay vessel, along with a piece of woollen cloth woven in a check pattern of dark brown and cream. The coins date the find to some time after AD230. That historic piece of tartan is now in the National Museum of Scotland at Edinburgh.

The first ever durable colour photograph was taken by a Scottish scientist, Edinburgh-born James Clerk Maxwell (1831-1879). His work on the field of optics and the study of colour vision created the foundation for practical colour photography, and in 1861 he demonstrated the world's first light-fast colour photograph – of a piece of tartan ribbon.

All things Scottish and tartan became highly fashionable in the 19th century, partly due to the huge popularity of the novels and poetry of the Scottish writer Sir Walter Scott (1771-1832). It was Sir Walter who orchestrated the visit of George IV to Edinburgh in 1822, the first reigning monarch to visit Scotland since Charles II in 1651. It was an occasion of plaided pageantry and King George attended a ball in full Highland dress, but rather spoiled the effect by wearing pink silk tights beneath his kilt. The immodestly short length of his kilt also excited comment, but as Lady Hamilton-Dalrymple dryly observed, 'Since he is to be among us for so short a time, the more we see of him the better.'

'A man in a kilt is a man and a half.'
Sir Colin Campbell (1792-1863), Brigadier-General of the 93rd ('Sutherland Highlanders')
Regiment of Foot

A MISCELLANY

During his lifetime Sir Walter Scott lived at several addresses in Edinburgh, the most famous being 39 Castle Street, where he wrote many of the Waverley novels. A major landmark of the city is the Scott Monument in Princes Street Gardens, which is the largest monument to a writer in the world. If you manage to climb up the 287 steps inside the monument to the viewing platform at the top, you can claim a certificate to prove it!

Another famous writer linked with the city was Edinburgh-born Robert Louis Stevenson (1850-1894). He based his successful novel 'The Strange Case of Dr Jekyll and Mr Hyde' about a man with a split personality, one good and one evil, on the character of Deacon Brodie, who was a respectable town councillor by day and a burglar by night. Brodie lived in what is now Brodie's Close, an alleyway off the Royal Mile in Edinburgh, and was eventually found out and executed in 1788.

EDINBURGH, PRINCES STREET AND THE SCOTT MONUMENT
1883 E24301

In the Palace Yard of Edinburgh Castle is the Scottish National War Memorial. This was originally unveiled in 1927 to commemorate nearly 150,000 Scottish casualties in the First World War, and the memorial depicts, in bronze and stained glass, every type of war service imaginable in that conflict, including the contribution of the transport mules, carrier pigeons, and even the mice and canaries used to detect gas in the mines and trenches of the Western Front. Since its unveiling, thousands more names have been added to the memorial's Roles of Honour, commemorating around 50,000 Scottish casualties from the Second World War, the Malayan Emergency, the Korean War, Northern Ireland, the Falklands War, the Gulf War and, sadly, more recent conflicts.

A gruesome item on display in the National Museum of Scotland in Edinburgh is the 'Scottish Maiden', an early form of guillotine which used to stand in the Grassmarket and was used for executions between 1564 and 1708. It was introduced to Scotland during the minority of James VI by the Regent, James Douglas, Earl of Morton – who, ironically, was himself beheaded on the contraption in 1581.

**EDINBURGH, THE CASTLE
FROM THE GRASSMARKET
1897** 39121

STIRLING CASTLE, THE GREAT HALL 2011 *(Photograph courtesy of Reef Television)*

Stirling Castle sits on a commanding and strategic position on top of a crag with cliffs on three sides, and is one of Scotland's largest and most important castles, both defensively and architecturally. Nearly all the castle buildings seen today were built between 1490 and 1600, when it was an important royal residence. This view shows the Great Hall (or Parliament Hall), one of the first examples of Renaissance architecture in the country, which was completed in 1503. It is the largest great hall in Scotland, and has been described as 'the greatest secular building erected in Scotland in the late Middle Ages'. In the 19th century Stirling Castle became a military barracks and the Great Hall was remodelled; many original features were removed, including the hammerbeam roof, but this historic building has now been fully restored to its medieval glory. A feature of its interior is the magnificent new oak hammerbeam roof, which was constructed without a single nail. The exterior of the hall has also been 'harled', as it used to be in medieval times, with a thick waterproofing layer of lime plaster applied to its surface.

SCOTLAND

One of Scotland's most iconic structures is the Forth Bridge, the cantilever railway bridge over the Firth of Forth that was originally built to carry the North British Railway's main line between Edinburgh and Aberdeen. It was designed by Sir John Fowler and Sir Benjamin Baker, and was the first major structure in Britain to be constructed in steel. Work began on the bridge in 1832 and it was officially opened on 4th March 1890. Of the workforce of 4,600 men who laboured on its construction, 63 were killed in work-related accidents, despite rescue boats stationed under the bridge which did save eight lives, and hundreds more were left crippled by serious accidents. The bridge has an overall length of 8,296 feet (2,529 metres) including the approach viaducts, the lofty steel cantilevers are supported on granite piers, and the railway tracks run across the bridge at 150 feet (46 metres) above sea level. The bridge is Scotland's largest listed structure, and it remains a vital part of the railway system, carrying up to 200 train movements a day.

THE FORTH BRIDGE
1897 39145

FALKIRK, THE FALKIRK WHEEL, THE GONDOLAS IN PERFECT BALANCE 2005 F248711

A more recent masterpiece of Scottish engineering is the 'Falkirk Wheel'. This impressive structure is the only rotating boat lift in the world, and connects the Union Canal with the Forth & Clyde Canal. The upper section is an aqueduct from which boats are 'brought down' 30 metres to the canal basin below. At the end of the aqueduct is a huge wheel, with one gondola at the top and another at the bottom. A boat moves into the top gondola and then the wheel rotates 180 degrees to transfer it down to the basin below. The Falkirk Wheel's simple design is based on the perfect poise of the two gondolas, using Archimedes' principle of water displacement. The water in the top and bottom gondolas is at the same level, so they both weigh the same, and each boat displaces its own weight of water, so the wheels always balance. The wheel transports boats from one canal to the other in 15 minutes – a lot quicker than the whole day it took to negotiate the flight of 11 locks that was there before!

SCOTLAND

Scotland has 7 officially recognised cities – Aberdeen, Dundee, Edinburgh, Glasgow, Inverness, Stirling, and Perth, which was granted city status in 2012 as part of Queen Elizabeth II's diamond jubilee celebrations. It was from the pulpit of St John's Kirk at Perth in 1559 that John Knox gave his famous sermon against idolatry, which many regard as the start of the religious Reformation in Scotland.

One of the finest medieval cathedrals in Scotland was at Elgin, but it ceased to be used after the Reformation and now only survives as a ruin. Amongst many interesting tombs around the ruins is a gravestone with this telling inscription:

'This world is a cite full of streets &
Death is the mercat that all men meets.
If life were a thing that monie could buy,
The poor could not live and the rich could not die.'

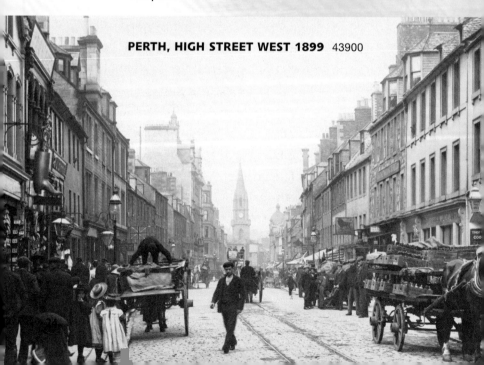

PERTH, HIGH STREET WEST 1899 43900

The largest cathedral ever built in Scotland in medieval times was at St Andrews, which housed relics of St Andrew, the patron saint of Scotland whose feast day is 30th November. St Andrew was a fisherman of Galilee and one of the twelve disciples of Christ; he was martyred in Greece by being crucified on an X-shaped cross formed of diagonal struts, the pattern which is seen today in the white diagonal cross on the blue background of the Saltire, Scotland's national flag. The relics made the cathedral at St Andrews an important place of pilgrimage in the Middle Ages, but its days of glory ended following three days of vigorous preaching by John Knox at Holy Trinity Church in St Andrews in June 1559. Fired up by Knox, a mob left the church and ransacked the cathedral, 'to purge the kirk and break down the altars and images and all kinds of idolatrie'. The cathedral was gradually looted of its riches, including the actual fabric of the building, and only its ruins stand now.

Glasgow Cathedral is the most complete medieval cathedral surviving in Scotland, having lost only its western towers which were dismantled in the 19th century, although 'cathedral' is purely an honorific title now, since it has not been the seat of a bishop since the late 17th century – its correct name is the High Kirk of Glasgow, and it hosts a congregation of the Church of Scotland. The Gothic structure that stands today was built between the late 12th and mid 15th centuries. Although it suffered damage during the Reformation, when it was attacked by religious zealots in 1560 to cleanse it of all traces of idolatry, the people of Glasgow held the building in such esteem that they helped fund its repair in 1574. Bullet holes can still be seen in the sacristy door of the cathedral, bearing witness to that troubled time in the history of this magnificent place of worship.

In April 2010 the title of the tallest tree in Scotland, and also in Britain, was awarded to the Ardkinglas Grand Fir in the Woodland Garden of the Ardkinglas Estate on the banks of Loch Fyne in Argyll, when its expertly measured height of 210 feet and 11 inches (64.28 metres) gave it the edge over the previous record holders, the Stronardon Douglas Fir near Dunans Castle in Argyll, and Dughall Mor ('Big Dougal') in Reelig Glen Wood near Inverness, also a Douglas Fir.

The oldest tree in Scotland is the Fortingall Yew that grows in a walled enclosure in the churchyard of Fortingall, near Aberfeldy in Perthshire. The ancient, twisted yew tree is probably around 2,000 years old, making it also one of the oldest living trees in Europe.

Scotland's longest river is the Tay, which flows for amost 120 miles from its source on the slopes of Ben Lui at the head of Glen Fyne before reaching the sea east of Dundee. Dundee used to be famous for its 'three Js' – jute, jam and journalism. The jute and jam industries are gone now, but journalism remains in the form of the D C Thomson publishing company. Its many publications include the children's comics the 'Dandy' (launched 1937) and the 'Beano' (launched 1938). Although the 'Dandy' is no longer produced in printed form (the final print edition was December 2012) it is still available as an online comic. One of its most popular characters is commemorated with the statue of Desperate Dan in the centre of Dundee.

Dundee also had an important linen industry in the 18th and early 19th centuries, using flax shipped in from the Baltic. During the Napoleonic Wars there was huge demand for Dundee-manufactured sailcloth and hammocks for the Royal Navy. In the archives at Dundee University is a piece of sailcloth from Admiral Lord Nelson's flagship the 'Victory', on which he died during the Battle of Trafalgar in 1805. The sails from important ships were often cut up to make souvenirs, but this piece is particularly interesting as it bears the maker's stamp – Baxter Bros from Dundee!

**DUNDEE, DESPERATE DAN
FROM THE 'DANDY' 2005**
D81718

BRAEMAR, CLEARING SNOW FROM THE CAIRNWELL PASS 1879 B266003

'There are two seasons in Scotland: June and winter.'

(Billy Connolly, Scottish comedian and actor, born 1942)

The lowest air temperature ever recorded in the UK is -27.2°C (-16.96°F), which has occurred not just once but three times – all in Scotland! The freezing temperature was recorded twice at Braemar in Aberdeenshire, on 11th February 1895 and 10th January 1982, and most recently at Altnaharra in Sutherland on 30th December 1995.

However, Scotland redeems itself by also being the location of the highest air temperature ever recorded in the UK, of 32.9°C (91.22°F) on 9th August 2003 at Greycrook, near St Boswells in the Scottish Borders.

'Scotch mist, n - a heavy wet mist of the type that is characteristically found in the Scottish Highlands and Islands.'

(Definition in 'The Penguin English Dictionary', 2002)

Despite the popular view that it rains a lot in Scotland, the precipitation rate varies widely across the country. The western Highlands and islands do indeed enjoy a lot of rain, around 118 inches (3,000mm) per year, but much of lowland Scotland receives an annual rainfall of less than 31.5 inches (800mm). However, Scotland has held the record for the most rain to fall in a 30-minute period in the UK since 26th June 1953, when 3.15 inches (80mm) fell on Eskdalemuir in Dumfries and Galloway in half an hour – what a lucky place.

Wherever rain falls, a Scotsman can be thanked for inventing the raincoat – in 1824, Glasgow chemist Charles Macintosh developed a process of rubber-proofing cloth which he used to manufacture the first raincoats. His contribution to the world is recalled in the names of 'macintosh' or 'mac' that are now common usage for any form of waterproof coat. Scotland has also given us the Inverness cape – a sleeveless coat with a shoulder cape serving as protection to the arms and upper body. It is often worn in rainy weather by pipe bands, and is famously associated with the fictional detective Sherlock Holmes.

Something you might enjoy when outdoors on a cold or wet day is a hot drink from a vacuum, or Thermos, flask. This was invented by Sir James Dewar (1842-1923), a brilliant physicist and chemist who was born at Kincardine in Fife and educated at the University of Edinburgh. Dewar developed the insulated flask in 1892 whilst researching the liquefaction of gases at very low temperature, to keep the liquid material he was studying cold for a long period, but he failed to realise the wider potential of his invention and never patented it. Its commercial value was recognised by two glassblowers in Germany in 1904, who saw how useful it would be for keeping drinks hot as well as cold; they named the flask 'Thermos' (from the Greek word 'therme', meaning heat) and successfully claimed the commercial rights to the product.

SCOTLAND

Scotland's most northerly city is Inverness, situated where the River Ness flows into the Moray Firth and gives the settlement its name – from the Gaelic 'Inbhir Nis', meaning 'mouth of the River Ness'. The river begins its seven mile journey to Inverness from the northern end of Loch Ness, which may or may not be the haunt of Nessie the monster, but is definitely the largest freshwater body in the UK in terms of its volume of water, due to its great length and depth – nearly double that in all the lakes of England and Wales combined! Scotland is also the location of deepest freshwater body in the UK, Loch Morar on the west coast near Mallaig, whose maximum depth of 1,017 feet (310 metres) exceeds the height of The Shard in London, Britain's tallest building, whilst the largest loch in Scotland in terms of its total surface area of 27.45 square miles is the beautiful Loch Lomond, north of Glasgow.

LOCH LOMOND, FROM INCHTAVANNACH c1880 L94301

CULZEAN CASTLE 1904 53151

The famous architect Robert Adam was born in 1728 at Kirkcaldy in Fife. One of his finest works in Scotland is Culzean Castle on the west coast south of Ayr. This magnificent mansion in mock-Gothic style was built in the 1770s, incorporating the tower of an earlier stronghold.

North of Culzean Castle on the A719 between Knoweside and Drumshang is the 'Electric Brae', where the configuration of the surrounding landscape causes a strange optical illusion. The inscription on the stone sign beside the road explains how this occurs: 'The Electric Brae, known locally as Croy Brae…runs the quarter mile from the bend overlooking Croy railway viaduct in the west (286 feet Above Ordnance Datum) to the wooded Craigencroy Glen (303 feet A.O.D.) to the east. Whilst there is this slope of 1 in 86 upwards from the bend to the Glen, the configuration of the land on either side of the road provides an optical illusion making it look as if the slope is going the other way. Therefore, a stationary car on the road with the brakes off will appear to move slowly uphill. The term 'Electric' dates from a time when it was incorrectly thought to be a phenomenon caused by electric or magnetic attraction within the Brae.'

AYR, THE WALLACE TOWER AND THE HIGH STREET 1900 46002

'Auld Ayr, wham ne'er a town surpasses,
For honest men and bonie lassies.'

(Robert Burns, 1759-1796, from 'Tam o' Shanter')

Ayr is famous for its links with Robert Burns (1759-1796), Scotland's 'national poet', who was born in a cottage at Alloway, to the south of the town. He immortalised many places around Ayr in his work, including the Brig o' Doon which features in his mock-epic poem 'Tam o' Shanter'. This was based on real people Burns knew who drank at what is now the Tam o' Shanter Inn in Ayr's High Street, Douglas Graham of Shanter Farm ('Tam') and his crony John Davidson of Kirkoswald ('Souter Johnnie'). In the poem, Tam spends far too long in the pub before making what becomes an eventful journey home to face his wife, tellingly described by Burns as his 'sulky, sullen dame' who is 'gathering her brows like gathering storm, nursing her wrath to keep it warm.'

In 1789 Robert Burns began work as an Excise Office in Dumfries, where he lodged at the Globe Inn prior to setting up home in the town with his family – you can still see two verses of poetry there that he inscribed on the window panes of his bedroom. He died in Dumfries in 1796, where his remains lie in a mausoleum in St Michael's Churchyard.

The lyrics of Robert Burns are a vivid mixture of the personal and the political, the heart and soul. He was a social and political animal and many of his poems reflect the keen sense of outrage he felt at the hypocrisies of the age. He also collected folk songs from around Scotland, although he often revised or adapted them, such as 'Auld Lang Syne'. The life and works of Robert Burns are celebrated in Scotland on Burns Night, 25th January (the anniversary of his birthday), with a special Burns Supper when traditional dishes are eaten, especially haggis, Scotland's most

**ROBERT BURNS
(1759-1796)**

famous dish. Haggis is rather like a large, oval-shaped sausage, made from a sheep's stomach stuffed with oatmeal and the minced or chopped parts of an animal which might otherwise be discarded, such as the heart, lungs and liver (the finest haggis uses liver from a deer, rather than a sheep). At Burns Suppers the haggis is brought in to the accompaniment of a piper, and placed ceremoniously before the chief guest. 'To a Haggis' by Robert Burns is then recited ('Fair fa' your honest sonsie face, great chieftain o' the puddin' race!'), and the haggis is toasted with drams of whisky before being eaten.

SCOTLAND

Many places in Scotland have nicknames reflecting incidents in their history or something they are famous for – here are a few examples:

Comrie, a village in the district of Perth and Kinross near Crieff, is known as the 'Shaky Toun' because its position on the Highland Boundary Fault line makes it one of the most geologically active areas in the UK, where earthquakes are recorded more often and to a higher intensity than anywhere else in the country.

Paisley was known by the nickname of 'Seestu' in its past, deriving from a characteristic manner of speech in the town, whose people had the habit of interjecting 'Seestu?' (ie 'Seest thou?', or 'Do you understand?') into their conversation.

East Kilbride enjoys the nickname of 'Polo Mint City' – after the round mint with a hole in the middle – because of the large number of roundabouts in its road system. It was immortalised as such in the song 'Polo Mint City' by the Scottish rock band Texas which appears on their album 'White on Blonde' of 1997.

Edinburgh was known as 'Auld Reekie' in the past, because the city always seemed to be blanketed with a cloud of 'reek', or smoke. In the 18th and 19th centuries new prosperity came to Edinburgh and much of its magnificent Georgian architecture was built during this 'Golden Age', making it a city of gracious squares and impressive public buildings that earned a new name, 'The Athens of the North'. Edinburgh has more listed buildings than anywhere else in the UK.

Kirkcaldy, on the south coast of Fife, is known as the 'The Lang Toun' because the main street of the early town stretched for nearly a mile along the coastline.

Dunfermline is known as 'The Auld Grey Toun' because of the grey stonework of many of its old buildings.

Kirriemuir is known as the 'Wee Red Toonie' after the red sandstone from which many of the town's older properties are built. Kirriemuir was the birthplace in 1860 of J M Barrie, the author and playwright who created 'Peter Pan' and immortalised Kirriemuir as 'Thrums' in his novels 'Auld Licht Idylls, 'A Window in Thrums' and 'The Little Minister'. J M Barrie's birthplace at 9 Brechin Road in Kirriemuir, together with the adjoining house, is now in the care of the National Trust of Scotland as a museum to his life and work, and a statue of Peter Pan stands in the town square.

Musselburgh has been known as 'The Honest Toun' since 1332, when the Regent of Scotland, Randolph, Earl of Moray, died in the burgh after a long illness. The citizens of the town cared for him so well and loyally during his illness that his successor as Regent, the Earl of Mar, offered them a reward – however, they declined, saying they had been doing no more than their duty. The impressed Earl declared that they were a set of honest men, and Musselburgh celebrates its reputation with its town motto, 'Honestas'.

Dumfries lies on the River Nith, where the old medieval sandstone bridge that spans the river was constructed in 1432 and is the oldest multiple-arched bridge in Scotland. Dumfries is affectionately known as 'Queen of the South', which is also the name of its football club. A proud boast of fans of Queen of the South FC is that it is the only football team to be named in the Bible: 'The Queen of the South shall rise again at the day of judgement' (Luke XI, 31).

SCOTLAND

Glasgow's origins date from the 6th century when St Mungo built a church where Glasgow Cathedral now stands. Its name probably comes from the Gaelic 'Glaschu', meaning 'the dear green place' – an apt name for the modern city, which has more parks and green spaces relative to its size than any other city in Europe. George Square was laid out in the 1780s and named in honour of George III. Its centrepiece is the tall column topped with a statue of the Scottish author Sir Walter Scott (1771-1832). The original plan was to have a statue of King George on the column, but the city fathers went off the idea because the loss of the American colonies during the king's reign saw the end of Glasgow's lucrative tobacco trade with North America and caused severe losses to its tobacco merchants, previously so wealthy that they were called 'Tobacco Lords'. Scott's statue represents him with a plaid draped over his right shoulder, obeying a convention which correctly identifies him as a native of the Borders, rather than as a Highlander.

GLASGOW, GEORGE SQUARE 1897 39759

Eleven other statues of famous 19th century figures stand in George Square, including one of a young Queen Victoria on horseback – the only equestrian statue of the queen that was ever made. Amongst the others, one commemorates Glasgow-born Thomas Graham (1805-1869), a graduate of the University of Glasgow who became a brilliant chemist and invented kidney dialysis, and James Watt (1737-1819), the great engineer who pioneered efficient steam engines, a vital factor in the success of Britain's Industrial Revolution. Although the Englishman Thomas Newcomen had developed the first practical steam engine, his design was very inefficient. It was Greenock-born James Watt who devised a way of improving their efficiency after being asked to repair a Newcomen engine whilst working as an instrument maker at Glasgow University. One day in 1765 he was crossing Glasgow Green when the idea of a separate condenser for the steam engine occurred to him, to reduce the consumption of fuel and steam. It could be said that the Industrial Revolution was born on Glasgow Green, and a commemorative engraved boulder marks the spot where James Watts had his flash of inspiration.

The world's first radiology department was set up in 1896 at the Royal Infirmary in the city by Glasgow-born Dr John Macintyre (1857-1928), who was the first person to use X-rays for diagnosis and treatment of patients.

Charles Rennie Mackintosh (1868-1928), was a famous Glasgow architect who evolved 'The Glasgow Style' at the turn of the 19th and 20th centuries, a middle point between Art Nouveau and Art Deco. Notable Glasgow buildings he designed are the Glasgow School of Art, the Scotland Street School (now the Scotland Street School Museum, telling the story of education in Scotland over a hundred years, from the late 19th century to the late 20th century) and Miss Cranston's Willow Tea Rooms at 217 Sauchiehall Street. His design for 'The House of an Art Lover', which won a German design competition in 1906, was realised in the 1990s and stands in Bellahouston Park.

FRASERBURGH, THE HERRING FLEET c1900 F63002

'Chasing the silver darlings...'

With Scotland's long coastline it is not surprising that fishing has been important to many Scottish communities over the years, ranging from small fishing villages to the great trawler port of Aberdeen, which was the biggest fishing port in the world until the early 20th century. Herring were a particularly important catch for Scottish fishermen in the past, who called them 'silver darlings', but hunting the herring was a perilous business for them because of the shallow-decked boats they favoured, as seen in this photograph of Fraserburgh where the harbour is crowded with open boats from ports around the region. The vessel in the foreground is from Nairn, further west along the Moray Firth, and is a Zulu, one of the finest fore-and mizzen-rigged lugger designs of the late 19th century. Though she is broad in the beam, her decking is shallow to allow drift nets laden with fish to be hauled on board easily, and would offer scant protection in the violent storms of the North Sea.

Once the catch had been landed, gutting and packing the fish into barrels was done by women. This was a skilled job, and a good herring woman could gut 40 fish a minute. It was essential for the women to keep their fingers nimble, which they did by continuously knitting in their free time.

This bonny lady was photographed at Coldingham, a few miles north-west of the Border fishing town of Eyemouth. An annual event at Eyemouth is the Herring Queen Festival every July, a week of colourful festivities celebrating the town's heritage as a fishing community. The highlight of the festival is the crowning of the Herring Queen after she has been brought into the harbour by boat with her maids of honour. In past years the Herring Queen had to be the daughter of a local fisherman, but now a panel of local people make the selection from nominees.

COLDINGHAM, A SCOTTISH FISH WIFE IN TRADITIONAL COSTUME c1932 C358024

Scotland

Aberdeen's association with North Sea oil and the use of its harbour and airport by the oil industry has given it the title of 'oil capital of Europe', but an older name is 'The Granite City', dating from the 18th and 19th centuries when it underwent a programme of expansion and redevelopment and many buildings were constructed from locally quarried granite, which sparkles in the sunshine. Two famous names from that time are John Smith (1781-1852) and Archibald Simpson (1790-1847), who designed much of the new centre of the city. One of Simpson's designs was the headquarters of the North of Scotland Bank, the corner building with pillars behind the market cross in this view. It was known as 'The Hinge of the City', because of its prominent position and also its shape – it is a brilliant solution to the problem (for neo-classical architecture) of an irregular angle between the streets. The curving entrance unites what are effectively two buildings, one on each street, topped with a statue of Demeter, the Greek goddess of plenty. The building is now a public house, named, appropriately, The Archibald Simpson after its designer, whose masterpiece this is.

**ABERDEEN
UNION STREET AND
THE MARKET CROSS
C1885** A90305

The chief thoroughfare of Aberdeen, Union Street was built from 1800 to 1805. It was so-named to commemorate the Act of Union of 1800 in which the Parliaments of Great Britain and Ireland were united.

Three important public buildings stand on a prominent site in the centre of Aberdeen, at the end of Union Terrace: the Central Library, St Mark's Church and His Majesty's Theatre. They are known locally as Education, Salvation and Damnation!

James Gibbs, one of Britain's greatest architects, was born in the Footdee (Fittie) area of Aberdeen in 1682. His best-known works are the Church of St Martin-in-the-Fields and St Bartholomew's Hospital in London, the Senate House for Cambridge University and the Radcliffe Camera for Oxford University. James Gibb returned home to Aberdeen in 1739 and gave his native city plans in the Italian style which were used for rebuilding the West Kirk of St Nicholas, off Union Street, which is also notable for housing the largest carillon in Britain, consisting of 48 bells.

In medieval times there was a wayside chapel at the south end of the ancient Brig o' Dee over the River Dee at Aberdeen, where people could pray before going on a journey. In the chapel was a painted wooden statue of the Virgin Mary. During the Reformation the statue, regarded as an idol, was thrown into the river and eventually floated out to sea where it was found by Catholic Flemish fishermen. They took it home to what is now Belgium, where it has remained ever since. After several moves, the statue is now kept in a small side chapel of the Catholic Church of Notre Dame du Finistère in Brussels, where it is known as Our Lady of Good Success, aka Our Lady of Aberdeen.

SCOTLAND

48 Skene Terrace in Aberdeen was once the home of the astronomer Sir David Gill (1834-1914), and he and the pioneer Aberdeen photographer George Washington Wilson took the first high definition photographs of the moon from there between 1868-69.

The first man to walk on the moon, in 1969, was the American astronaut Neil Armstrong (1930-2012), who had Scottish ancestry. In 1972 Neil Armstrong visited Langholm in Dumfries and Galloway, the traditional seat of Clan Armstrong, where he was given a hero's welcome and made the first Freeman of the burgh. Langholm also used to be famous for its annual Handfasting Fair, where unmarried couples joined hands before witnesses and agreed to live together for a year; they returned to the fair the next year and if the handfasting had been successful they were married – if not, they agreed to part.

South of Langholm is Gretna Green, which became popular for the marriages of runaway English couples after 'irregular' marriages were abolished in England in 1754 but not in Scotland, and the construction of a toll road in the 1770s made it the first easily reachable town over the Scottish border. 'Irregular' marriages required neither banns nor licence, as long as the declaration was made before two witnesses; almost anybody had authority to conduct a declaratory marriage, and the local blacksmiths (known as 'anvil priests') famously performed them over their anvils. Gretna Green's history has made the area very popular for weddings, and thousands of couples marry there each year with a service performed over an iconic blacksmith's anvil as an additional romantic touch.

The minimum legal age for marriages in Britain was 12 for a girl and 14 for a boy until it was raised to 16 in 1929. Parental consent for a marriage is required until the age of 18 in England and Wales, but in Scotland no parental consent is required from the age of 16.

Moffat is a historic spa town in the Annandale valley of Dumfries and Galloway. In the High Street is The Famous Star Hotel – why 'famous'? It is officially listed in the Guinness Book of Records as being the world's narrowest hotel, at only 20 feet (6 metres) wide!

Another Scottish town with a place in Guinness Book of Records is Wick in Caithness, where Ebenezer Place at the junction of Union Street and River Street was officially recognised in 2006 as the world's shortest street. With a total length of 6 feet 9 inches (2.06 metres), Ebenezer Place has only one address – the front door of No 1 Bistro, which is part of Mackays Hotel. The street originated in 1883, when 1 Ebenezer Place was constructed and the owner of the building was instructed to paint a name on its shortest side, and was officially declared a street in 1887.

The border between Scotland and England runs for 96 miles from just north of Berwick-upon-Tweed on the east coast and the Solway Firth on the west. It was defended and fought over for centuries, frequently crossed by invading forces from England and just as frequently crossed by Scottish armies and raiders heading south. One of the most disputed places in Scottish/English territory in the past was Berwick-upon-Tweed, where the River Tweed meets the sea after flowing along much of the Anglo-Scottish border. The town changed hands between England and Scotland 13 times between 1147 and 1482, since when it has been firmly in England. Berwick now lies 2½ miles south of the border, but its football team, Berwick Rangers FC, plays in the Scottish Football League – it is the only English football team to do so, so it is also the only Scottish league team to play its home fixtures on English ground.

HAWICK, THE 1514 MEMORIAL c1955 H248002

One of the largest towns of the Border region is Hawick, where the 1514 Memorial in the High Street commemorates the callants, or youths, of the town who defeated an English raiding party at Hornshole in 1514 and carried their captured flag back to the town in triumph. The event is also celebrated every June in the Hawick Common Riding, when several hundred horse-riders proceed around the town's marches, or boundaries, in a series of staged rides with a chosen flag-bearer, the Cornet, heading the main procession.

Many other Border towns celebrate their history with a Common Riding over the summer. These include the Selkirk Common Riding, the Jedburgh Callant's Festival and the Braw Lad's Gathering at Galashiels. The Galashiels event commemorates the town receiving its burgh charter in 1599, but a highlight of the Gathering is the Braw Lad, with the burgh flag flying, leading his riders to the Raid Stone that marks the place where men from Gala defeated a party of English raiders in 1337. The raiders were ambushed whilst they were picking wild plums, hence the town's motto of 'Sour Plums'.

A Miscellany

It wasn't just English raiders who harried the Border area in the past
– so too did lawless bands of bandits, cattle thieves and outlaws.
Known as reivers or moss-troopers, they fought out their own feuds,
murdered and plundered, ran protection rackets, organised armed
raids, and hired themselves out as assassins or kidnappers, owing
their loyalty only to the criminal gangs and families they belonged to.
It is from this time that the phrase 'Jedburgh justice' originates, also
known as 'Jedwood Justice' or 'Jeddart Justice', which means putting
someone to death and trying them afterwards – it derives from the
Border town of Jedburgh, where this sort of justice was dealt to
raiders and moss-troopers, who were hanged without trial.

Despite its turbulent past, Scotland's Border country is now a
peaceful land of beautiful hill scenery, watered by rivers such as the
Tweed, Teviot, Yarrow and Jed, and watched over by the picturesque
ruins of magnificent medieval abbeys like Dryburgh, Jedburgh, Kelso
and Melrose – where the heart of Robert the Bruce was buried.

MELROSE, THE ABBEY 1897 39192

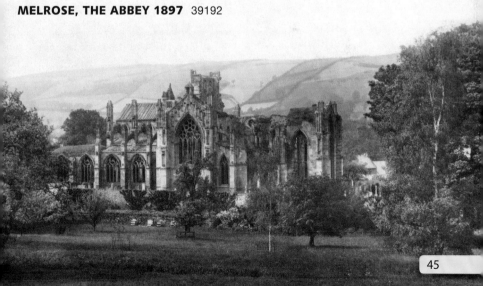

Sporting Scotland

Scotland is famous as the home of golf, which originated from 'gowf', a game first played on the eastern coast of Fife in the mid 14th century. Golf became so popular in medieval Scotland that in 1457 James II banned the sport, because it was distracting young men from their archery practice and reducing church attendance. Fortunately for modern golfers, James IV became a convert of the game and from 1502 the sport was revived under royal patronage. The oldest verifiable golf club in the world is The Honourable Company of Edinburgh Golfers, founded in 1744, whose headquarters has been the championship course at Muirfield in East Lothian since 1891. The ruling authority on the game is The Royal and Ancient Golf Club at St Andrews which was founded in 1754, although golf has been played on the links at St Andrews since the 14th century, where the Old Course is the oldest golf course in the world.

Water polo was invented in Scotland. A form of the sport was first played at Aberdeen in the 1870s by members of the Bon Accord Swimming Club, after its president asked William Wilson, president of the ASCS and manager at Glasgow's Victoria Baths Club, to devise a diversion to add interest to the club's annual championships gala. He came up with a set of rules for a game of 'aquatic football' which was played from bank to bank of the River Dee. Wilson later revised and improved the rules for the sport he had devised, and the first game played in a pool under these new conditions took place in Glasgow in 1879. Subsequently the Scottish rules were adopted worldwide in the early years of the sport.

The Scottish Grand National is held at Ayr Racecourse, which is one of the premier venues for horseracing in Scotland – another important fixture in its calendar is the Ayr Gold Cup, the richest sprint handicap in Europe.

The Musselburgh Silver Arrow is competed for annually by the Royal Company of Archers, an archery club that has a ceremonial role as the Sovereign's Bodyguard in Scotland. It dates back to 1603, and is believed to be the oldest sporting trophy in the UK.

Shinty (or 'camanachd' in its Gaelic form) is Scotland's oldest national sport, and has probably been played in the country since the sixth century. It is a fast-moving team game played with curved sticks and a ball that is similar to the Irish game of hurling, and a forebear of the modern game of hockey. Highland emigrants to Canada continued to play shinty on the frozen lakes and, generations later, the game developed into ice hockey.

Another sport that originated in medieval Scotland is curling, a game with rules similar to bowls. Two teams of four players take turn to slide thick, polished stone discs across a sheet of flat ice towards a circular target area. The curler can induce the stone to turn slowly as its slides, and its path can be further influenced by two sweepers with brooms who brush the ice in front of the stone as it slides. It used to be played on frozen lochs and ponds, but nowadays it is played on indoor ice rinks. Curling travelled overseas with Scottish emigrants, and is now particularly popular in Canada. In 1998 it became an official sport in the Winter Olympics.

Traditional Highland Games meetings take place in many places in Scotland each year. The events include tug-of-war, putting the stone, throwing the Scottish hammer and tossing the caber, which is a long, heavy pole or tree trunk. The competitor must toss the caber upwards and away from him so that the end in his hands completes a 180-degree arc and lands at the 12 o'clock position.

One of Scotland's most unusual sporting events takes place on Easdale Island, one of the Slate Islands off the west coast in the Firth of Lorn, where a disused slate quarry is the venue for the World Stone Skimming Championships held each year on the last Sunday in September – anyone of any age or level of skill can enter.

SCOTLAND

QUIZ QUESTIONS

Answers on page 50.

1. What is known as 'the Scottish Verdict?

2. What and where is 'The Hollow Mountain'?

3. Which building in Glasgow is nicknamed 'The Armadillo'?

4. The following are nicknames for inhabitants of which Scottish places?
   a) Doonhamers. b) Teries. c) Habbies. d) Hearachs.

5. Many golfers dream of playing a round at the famous Old Course at St Andrews. Before the number of holes on the Old Course was reduced to 18, creating what became the standard for golf courses throughout the world, it had how many – 20, 22 or 24?

6. What are 'The Scottish Munros'?

7. The small island of Ailsa Craig in the Firth of Clyde is said to provide the best granite for making – what?

8. By what name are these Scottish football clubs better known?
   a) The Caley-Jags. b) The Red Lichties. c) The Sons. d) The Pars.
   e) The Steelmen. f) The Bairns.

9. A 'tattie bogle' is the Scots term for – what?

10. One of Scotland's traditional dishes is Cullen Skink – what is it?

A Miscellany

TROSSACHS
A HOTEL AND LOCH ACHRAY
1899 44603

QUIZ ANSWERS

1. Scotland has its own legal system, separate from that of England and Wales, with a basis derived from Roman law. Under Scottish law, juries in a criminal trial can return one of three possible verdicts, as opposed to the usual two: 'guilty', 'not guilty' and – uniquely – 'not proven', which is sometimes called 'the Scottish Verdict'. Both the 'not guilty' and 'not proven' verdicts result in an acquittal with no possibility of retrial.

2. Ben Cruachan, overlooking Loch Awe in Argyll and Bute, is known as 'The Hollow Mountain' because concealed deep within its heart is a 400 megawatt pumped-storage hydroelectric power station, in a massive man-made cavern. Creating the cavern, the size of a football pitch, involved the excavation of over 220,000 cubic metres of rock and soil. There is a visitor centre at the outflow to Loch Awe.

3. The Clyde Auditorium at Glasgow is a concert venue that is popularly known as 'The Armadillo'. It lies on the north bank of the Clyde adjacent to the Scottish Exhibition and Conference Centre. Designed by the eminent architect Sir Norman Foster, it was completed in 1997 and has become one of the most iconic modern buildings of Glasgow.

GLASGOW, THE CLYDE AUDITORIUM 2005 G11719

4. a) Dumfries – from 'down homers'. b) Hawick – the name comes from a traditional song that includes the line 'Teribus ye teri odin', supposed to have been the war cry of the men of Hawick at the Battle of Flodden in 1513. c) Kilbarchan – after Habbie Simpson (1550-1620), a famous left-handed piper from the town; a statue of him stands in a niche in The Steeple in Kilbarchan's High Street. d) Harris, the southern part of Lewis and Harris, the largest island in the Outer Hebrides.

5. 22.

6. Scottish mountains with a height over 3,000 feet (914.4 metres). They are named after Sir Hugh Munro who published the first Munro Tables 1891, listing 280 peaks in Scotland above that height. The list is regularly revised, and there are currently 282 peaks in Scotland recognised as 'Munros', according to the 2012 revision published by the Scottish Mountaineering Club.

7. Curling stones, or 'rocks', the thick discs of polished granite used in the Scottish game of curling.

8. a) Inverness Caledonian Thistle FC. b) Arbroath FC.
   c) Dumbarton FC. d) Dunfermline Athletic FC.
   e) Motherwell FC. f) Falkirk FC.

9. A scarecrow.

10. Cullen Skink is a rich, creamy soup, rather like a chowder, made with smoked haddock and potatoes. There's a recipe for it on the next page.

RECIPE

CULLEN SKINK

Cullen Skink is a traditional Scottish recipe from the Moray Firth for a rich, creamy soup made with smoked haddock. 'Skink' comes from a Gaelic word which originally meant 'essence', but now describes a stew-like soup, whilst 'cullen' was the name for the 'seatown' (port or harbour) district of a town.

700g/1½ lbs smoked haddock (the un-dyed variety is best to use)
600ml/1 pint milk
600ml/1 pint water
2 onions, peeled – chop one onion and leave the other whole
1 blade of mace
50g/2oz butter
3 medium-sized potatoes, peeled and chopped into chunks
Salt and freshly ground black pepper
4 tablespoonfuls single cream
Chopped fresh parsley or chives, to garnish

Place the fish in a large saucepan, cover with the milk and water and add the whole onion and the mace. Bring slowly to the boil over a gentle heat, then reduce the heat and simmer very gently for 5 minutes. Remove the pan from the heat and leave to stand for 10 minutes. Strain off the cooking liquid and reserve.

In another saucepan, melt the butter, add the chopped onion and chopped potatoes and cook over a gentle heat for about 10 minutes, stirring occasionally, until the onion has started to soften. Pour the reserved, strained cooking liquid into the pan and simmer gently, until the potato pieces are soft. Remove from the heat and allow to cool slightly, then pass through a sieve or liquidize in a blender. Rinse out the saucepan, then return the liquidized soup to it.

Flake the cooked fish, being careful to remove all the bones and the skin, and stir the fish flesh into the soup. Add salt and freshly ground black pepper to taste, stir in the cream and reheat gently before serving. Serve with a garnish of finely chopped fresh parsley or chives.

RECIPE

CRANACHAN

This is one of Scotland's most delicious desserts, and features the raspberries that Scotland is famous for. The raspberries produced in Scotland are renowned for their flavour, due to their slow ripening in the cool Scottish summers. The main areas of what is regarded by many as Scotland's 'national fruit' are in Tayside, especially the Strathmore valley, but raspberries are also cultivated commercially in Grampian, the Highlands, Arran, the Borders and Ayrshire, which is noted for particularly fine fruit. Scotland is also the home of the tayberry, a large conical berry with a bright purple colour and a rich flavour, which was developed at the Scottish Crops Research Institute by crossing a raspberry with a blackberry.

> 50g/2oz medium oatmeal
> 4 tablespoonfuls clear runny honey
> 3 tablespoonfuls whisky
> 300ml/ ½ pint double cream
> 350g/12oz raspberries

Toast the oatmeal in a shallow layer on a sheet of foil under the grill for a few minutes, stirring occasionally, until it is evenly browned but not burnt. Leave to cool. Whip the cream in a large bowl until soft peaks form, then use a large metal spoon to gently fold in the oats, honey and whisky until well combined.

Reserve a few raspberries for decoration, then layer the remainder with the oat mixture in four serving dishes. Cover and chill for 2 hours.

About 30 minutes before serving, transfer the glasses to room temperature. Decorate with the reserved raspberries and serve.

FRANCIS FRITH

PIONEER VICTORIAN PHOTOGRAPHER

Francis Frith, founder of the world-famous photographic archive, was a complex and multi-talented man. A devout Quaker and a highly successful Victorian businessman, he was philosophical by nature and pioneering in outlook. By 1855 he had already established a wholesale grocery business in Liverpool, and sold it for the astonishing sum of £200,000, which is the equivalent today of over £15,000,000. Now in his thirties, and captivated by the new science of photography, Frith set out on a series of pioneering journeys up the Nile and to the Near East.

INTRIGUE AND EXPLORATION

He was the first photographer to venture beyond the sixth cataract of the Nile. Africa was still the mysterious 'Dark Continent', and Stanley and Livingstone's historic meeting was a decade into the future. The conditions for picture taking confound belief. He laboured for hours in his wicker dark-room in the sweltering heat of the desert, while the volatile chemicals fizzed dangerously in their trays. Back in London he exhibited his photographs and was 'rapturously cheered' by members of the Royal Society. His reputation as a photographer was made overnight.

VENTURE OF A LIFE-TIME

By the 1870s the railways had threaded their way across the country, and Bank Holidays and half-day Saturdays had been made obligatory by Act of Parliament. All of a sudden the working man and his family were able to enjoy days out, take holidays, and see a little more of the world.

With typical business acumen, Francis Frith foresaw that these new tourists would enjoy having souvenirs to commemorate their days out. For the next thirty years he travelled the country by train and by pony and trap, producing fine photographs of seaside resorts and beauty spots that were keenly bought by millions of Victorians. These prints were painstakingly pasted into family albums and pored over during the dark nights of winter, rekindling precious memories of summer excursions. Frith's studio was soon supplying retail shops all over the country, and by 1890 F Frith & Co had become the greatest specialist photographic publishing company in the world, with over 2,000 sales outlets, and pioneered the picture postcard.

FRANCIS FRITH'S LEGACY

Francis Frith had died in 1898 at his villa in Cannes, his great project still growing. By 1970 the archive he created contained over a third of a million pictures showing 7,000 British towns and villages.

Frith's legacy to us today is of immense significance and value, for the magnificent archive of evocative photographs he created provides a unique record of change in the cities, towns and villages throughout Britain over a century and more. Frith and his fellow studio photographers revisited locations many times down the years to update their views, compiling for us an enthralling and colourful pageant of British life and character.

We are fortunate that Frith was dedicated to recording the minutiae of everyday life. For it is this sheer wealth of visual data, the painstaking chronicle of changes in dress, transport, street layouts, buildings, housing and landscape that captivates us so much today, offering us a powerful link with the past and with the lives of our ancestors.

Computers have now made it possible for Frith's many thousands of images to be accessed almost instantly. The archive offers every one of us an opportunity to examine the places where we and our families have lived and worked down the years. Its images, depicting our shared past, are now bringing pleasure and enlightenment to millions around the world a century and more after his death.

For further information visit: www.francisfrith.com

FREE PRINT OF YOUR CHOICE

+ £2.63 POSTAGE

Choose any Frith photograph in this book.
Simply complete the Voucher opposite and
return it with your remittance for £2.63
(to cover postage) and we will print the
photograph of your choice in SEPIA (size 11 x
8 inches) and supply it in a cream mount with a
burgundy rule line (overall size 14 x 11 inches).
**Please note: photographs with a reference number
starting with a "Z" are not Frith photographs and
cannot be supplied under this offer.**
Offer valid for delivery to UK one address only.

Mounted Print

Overall size 14 x 11 inches (355 x 280mm)

PLUS: **Order additional Mounted Prints at
HALF PRICE - £10.00 each** (normally £20.00)
If you would like to order more Frith prints
from this book, possibly as gifts for friends and
family, you can buy them at half price (with no
additional postage costs).

PLUS: **Have your Mounted Prints framed**
For an extra £19.50 per print you can have your
mounted print(s) framed in an elegant polished
wood and gilt moulding, overall size
16 x 13 inches (no additional postage required).

> IMPORTANT!
>
> These special prices are only
> available if you use this form to
> order. You must use the ORIGINAL
> VOUCHER (no copies permitted).
>
> We can only despatch to one
> UK address. This offer cannot be
> combined with any other offer.

For further information about local books, please contact:localbooks@uberdistribution.co.uk

As a customer your name & address will be stored by Frith but not sold or rented to third parties.
Your data will be used for the purpose of this promotion only.

FRITH PRODUCTS AND SERVICES

All Frith photographs are available for you to buy as framed or mounted prints.
From time to time, other illustrated items such as Address Books and Maps are also
available. Already, almost 80,000 Frith archive photographs can be viewed and
purchased on the internet through the Frith website.

For more detailed information on Frith companies and products, visit:

www.francisfrith.com

For further information, or trade enquiries, contact:

The Francis Frith Collection, 6 Oakley Business Park, Wylye Road, Dinton, Wiltshire SP3 5EU

Tel: +44 (0) 1722 716 376 Fax: +44 (0) 1722 716 881 Email: sales@francisfrith.co.uk

Voucher

for FREE and Reduced Price Frith Prints

Do not photocopy this voucher. Only the original is valid, so please fill it in, cut it out and return it to us with your order.

	Picture ref no	Page number	Qty	Mounted @ £10.00	Framed + £19.50	Orders Total £
1			1	Free of charge*	£	£
2				£10.00	£	£
3				£10.00	£	£
4				£10.00	£	£
5				£10.00	£	£
6				£10.00	£	£

Please allow 28 days for delivery. Offer available to one UK address only

* Postage		£2.63
Total Order Cost		£

Title of this book . . . .

I enclose a cheque / postal order for £ . . . .
payable to 'The Francis Frith Collection'

OR debit my Mastercard / Visa / Maestro / Amex card

Card Number

Issue No (Maestro only)   Valid from (Maestro)

Card Security No   Expires

Signature

Name Mr/Mrs/Ms . . . .

Address . . . .

. . . .

. . . .

. . . . .Postcode. . . . .

Daytime Tel No . . . .

E-mail . . . .

Voucher Code: SS1   Valid to 31/12/15